MISSY MOO
the Highland Coo

Written & Illustrated by Kelsey Marshalsey

BROWN PAPER FOX
PUBLISHING

BROWN PAPER FOX
Cambridge, Ontario, Canada

www.brownpaperfox.com

Library and Archives Canada Cataloguing in Publication

Kelsey Marshalsey,author & illustrator
Missy Moo The Highland Coo / by Kelsey Marshalsey ;
illustrated by Kelsey Marshalsey
ISBN (978-1-7389133-1-2) (paperback book)
1. Children's books, English--Texts. 2.Cows--Rhyming.
3. Inspirations & Personal Growth. 4. Highland Cows--Children's Books.

First published by Brown Paper Fox, 2024
This edition published by Brown Paper Fox in 2024

To Ewan for continuing to help me with telling our stories,
and to Isla - our very own Missy Moo.

In the hills of green
where the cows love to roam,
was one fluffy cow
who called this pasture a home.

This one cow was known
as a Highland Coo,
happy and carefree,
they called her Missy Moo.

Her coat was so shaggy,
a mix of brown and red,

A messy crown of curls
sat on top of her head.

While other cows grazed
in fields, all the same,
Missy Moo stood out,
making life a fun game.

She danced in the meadows,
her hooves light as air,
a sight to behold,
she danced without care.

She danced on the newly
snow-covered ground,
new adventures in winter,
she had quickly found.

She danced when the clouds
dropped puddles of rain,
never bothered at all,
she did not complain.

As seasons changed,
and the days rolled by,
Missy Moo's spirit soared
high in the sky.

They would visit the brook,
with waters so clear,
reflections of Missy Moo,
such a vision, so dear.

While the others sipped quietly,
Missy Moo splashed and played,
in her own little world,
that she had made.

The other cows stared,
their eyes full of surprise,
as Missy Moo twirled,
under the wide-open skies.

One day Missy Moo started to sing
a sweet song,
the others fought the urge
not to sing along.

The cows all joined in,
a chorus so grand,
as Missy Moo led the tune,
across their green land.

Smiles stretched across faces,
a new friend was made.

She had shown them the fun
in never being afraid.

Different and special,
she's a coo full of cheer,
in the hearts of her friends,
forever held dear.

So remember to
embrace what makes you,

YOU,

just like our friend,
Missy Moo,
the Highland Coo.

Printed in the USA
CPSIA information can be obtained
at www.ICGtesting.com
LVHW070725061224
798379LV00013B/99
* 9 7 8 1 7 3 8 9 1 3 3 1 2 *